2014

merry Christmas, Marissa
Saw this little Book
and thought of you . . . . .
all Kinds of ideas
I Know you so enjoy!

love you
Sweetie,
Mary
xox

© 2002 by Barbour Publishing, Inc.

ISBN 1-58660-653-0

Cover image © PhotoDisc

Published by Humble Creek, P.O. Box 719, Uhrichsville, Ohio 44683

Printed in China.
5 4

Christmas at Home
HOLIDAY
GIFT IDEAS

Compiled by
Ellyn Sanna

HUMBLECREEK
INSPIRATION FOR LIFE

The gift of God is
eternal life in Christ Jesus our Lord.

ROMANS 6:23

Sometimes we get so caught up in the hustle and bustle of Christmas shopping that we forget what it's really all about. Shopping for our friends and family becomes one more burden at a time when we're already pressured for time.

Truth is, though, we give Christmas gifts to honor the birthday of the One who gave us so much: Jesus Christ. He is the ultimate Gift of the Father, and each small human gift we give is but a tiny reflection of God's great love. So this year, each time you shop or bake or sew, try remembering the reason why you're giving.

This book will give you some ideas for gifts that don't have to cost a lot of money. Remember—the money we spend or the effort we make isn't what counts; the only thing that matters is whether the gifts come from our hearts.

ELLYN SANNA, EDITOR

Homemade Gifts

God loves a cheerful giver. . . .
Your generosity will result in
thanksgiving to God.

2 CORINTHIANS 9:7, 11

Scented Cinnamon Ornaments

Line small baskets with Christmas tissue paper and put three or four ornaments in each basket for an inexpensive, fragrant gift. But don't eat!

> 1 cup cinnamon (cheaper if bought in bulk)
> ¾ cup applesauce
> 1 tbsp cloves
> 1 tbsp nutmeg
> 2 tbsps white glue

Combine ingredients, then work mixture two to three minutes until the dough is smooth. Roll out to ¼-inch thickness. Cut dough with floured cookie cutters. Using a straw or toothpick, make small holes in the tops of the ornaments, then place cutouts on wire racks and allow to dry for several days (turn over once each day). Thread red or green ribbon through holes and tie in a loop.

Victorian Hand Ornaments

Have a friend who would be uncomfortable if you bought them an expensive gift? And yet you want to let them know how much they mean to you. These ornaments make lovely, inexpensive gifts that say you care.

MATERIALS:
2 7 x 5-inch squares unbleached muslin
1 7 x 5-inch square fusible fleece interlinings
off-white thread
8-inch length of narrow ecru satin ribbon
30 inches of 2-inch wide ecru lace
silk rosebuds or dried baby's breath
sprays of dried evergreen

TOOLS/EQUIPMENT:
pins   iron   sewing machine
needle and thread   hot glue gun

Trace your hand (with closed fingers) onto one of the unbleached muslin squares. Fuse the fleece onto the other square of muslin. Pin the two squares together, right sides together, and machine stitch along the pattern lines, leaving the wrist end open. Clip the curves and turn right side out; press with hot iron. Machine stitch finger lines through all three layers. Turn the cuff end under and tuck the ends of a ribbon loop inside for the hanger; machine stitch. Cut the lace into three ten-inch lengths and with a needle and thread gather and hand sew to the top of the cuff. Place the remaining two lengths side by side, overlapping edges by $1/4$ inch, and sew together, then gather to form a rosette and attach to cuff. With a hot glue gun fasten rosebuds, baby's breath, and evergreen to the center of the rosette.

Fancy Sneakers

Buy plain white sneakers from a craft store or a discount department store. Use a hot glue gun to decorate with buttons, ribbon rosebuds, lace, and ribbons. Or use fabric paint to stencil designs. A one-of-a-kind gift for adults or children.

Button Earrings

Another easy and one-of-a-kind gift.

At your fabric store, buy interesting buttons with diameters of about one inch, the kind that have a loop on the back. Remove loop with a small knife. Hot glue to earring pieces (available at your craft store).

Button Frames

Individualize an inexpensive picture frame by using a glue gun to attach old buttons of different shapes and sizes all around the wooden frame. If you're including a photo with your gift (for instance, the kids' school pictures), color coordinate the buttons to match the picture.

Barrettes

These make wonderful gifts for little girls who are just getting interested in "looking pretty."

At your craft store buy a package of three-inch spring clasp barrettes. Use a hot glue gun to decorate these. Almost anything will work—brightly colored buttons, shoelaces, plastic stars, painted wooden shapes, shells, silk flowers, bright balloons, even small toy pieces like Legos or puzzle pieces. Use your imagination and have fun!

Wreaths

Everyone can use one more wreath—and busy working folk are glad to at last have one to put on their door!

Buy a plain, undecorated wreath and decorate it yourself. Use your imagination—or attach any of the items listed below:

plaid Christmas ribbons
bunches of baby's breath
pine cones
sprays of wheat or dried grass

tiny tree decorations
lace
dried or silk flowers

Avoid the
Christmas Rush

It's too late for this year—but next year, why not sit down in January and make a list of all the people you want to remember at Christmastime? Think about what gifts you'd like to make, and get started with the new year. If you make a few gifts each month, by the time December comes again, you'll already have most of your gifts waiting to be given—and you'll have time to enjoy Advent as a season of holy love, rather than a season of exhausted busyness.

For Those Short on Time

The Lord Jesus himself said:
"It is more blessed to give
than to receive."

ACTS 20:35

Containers of Food

Even if you don't bake, you can still give food as gifts. Buy in bulk and personalize your gifts by packing them in a unique container (for instance, a flower pot, mixing bowl, mason jar, antique tin, decorative glass jar, etc.). That way the container becomes part of the gift—and you don't have to spend an arm and a leg if you pick things up all year at flea markets and yard sales. Fill your containers with fresh coffee beans, tea, nuts, Christmas M&Ms or other candy (such as chocolate-covered raisins), seasonings, pasta, or dried fruit.

Small Christmas Tree

Here's a gift that's great for someone in a nursing home or the hospital. Or it's a thoughtful gift for someone who lives alone and may not "bother" with a tree.

Buy a small, live Norfolk pine. Decorate with small balls, tiny wooden ornaments, red wooden bead garland, and a small star on top.

Gift Certificates

These make wonderful and welcome gifts for neighbors, teachers, employees, and friends, giving them a chance to pamper themselves in ways they might not otherwise. You can purchase gift certificates almost everywhere: the mall, restaurants, theaters, spas, beauty salons, music stores, athletic stadiums, etc.—as well as from gift and specialty catalogs. If you know a person's general interests, a gift certificate allows you to leave the individual choices to that person rather than having to guess whether or not they have a particular item.

Dress-Up Trunk

This is one of the best gifts ever for any child!

Go to your local Salvation Army thrift store, church rummage room, or St. Vincent de Paul's. Buy enough interesting old clothes to fill a good-size box—long, lace formals, old men's suits, high heels, scarves, jewelry, fancy hats, etc. Pack your finds in a box—you could buy a large plastic storage box, but a cardboard box works just as well. Decorate the box with stickers, the child's name in tape, etc. (Use your imagination!)

Stocking Stuffers

"If you, then. . .
know how to give good gifts
to your children,
how much more will your Father
in heaven give good gifts
to those who ask him!"

MATTHEW 7:11

For the Tea Drinker

antique teacup
individual packets of different flavored teas
small boxes of cookies
tea strainer
quilted tea cozy

For the Coffee Lover

coffee mug
reusable filter
small coffee bean grinder
travel mug (insulated)

small bags of assorted
flavors of coffee
gift certificate to a
specialty coffee store

For a Young Woman

scented soaps
sponges
small cosmetic bag
hair accessories
gift certificate
   to a salon/day spa
scented shampoo/conditioner

loofah
scented lotions
sample-size cosmetics
nail polish
jewelry
nail files

For a Young Man

pocket calculator
Walkman radio
small high-power flashlight
tickets to a sporting event
books on sports/activities
   of interest

pens
notepads
pocket watch
   (inexpensive
   battery kind)

For the Cook

measuring spoons

wooden spoons

jars of spices

whisks of various sizes

kitchen timer

recipe book

various shapes
  for cutout cookies

measuring cups

small grater

tiny food processor

spatulas

candy thermometer

recipe holder/box

small bowls

Tupperware containers

For the Student

pens
small notepads
paper clips
stapler
computer discs
thesaurus
highlighters

pencils
Post-its in various sizes
and colors
fun mouse pad
pocket-size dictionary
bookmarks

For the New (or Expectant) Mother

pacifiers

sample-size bottles of
   baby lotion, baby oil,
   baby powder

rattles

teething rings

brush for cleaning bottles

purse-size package of
   baby wipes

baby monitor

bibs

tape or CD of lullabies

bottles

baby booties/slippers

handmade coupons for free baby-sitting in the months to come

For the Cat
(or the Cat Lover)

nail clipper
catnip bags
jingly balls
collar
food/water bowl

brush for grooming
toy mouse
book about cat care
personalized tags
bag of cat treats

For the Dog
(or the Dog Lover)

Milkbones
ball
nail clipper
dog frisbee
collar
personalized tags

rawhide chews
brush for grooming
book about dog care
squeaky toy
leash

Party
Favors

Share with God's people. . . .
Practice hospitality.

ROMANS 12:13

Candles

A single candle set at each place, tied with a bit of curly holiday ribbon, makes a fragrant holiday gift your guests can enjoy in their own homes. Or you might put the candles in a basket by your door and ask that each guest take one as they leave.

Fresh Fruit

At each place, set a small wicker basket filled with inexpensive and brightly colored fruit: mandarin oranges, tangerines, or apples. Decorate the basket with a holiday bow.

Crackers

Victorian England gave us this Christmas tradition: paper "crackers" that contained small toys, jokes, or paper crowns. You can order authentic English crackers from many gift catalogs, and they'll come complete with a small toy inside. Or you can make your own.

Cover toilet paper tubes with red or green satin. You can add ribbons, embroidery, or silk flowers to makes your "crackers" even more festive. Tie the ends with lengths of curly Christmas ribbon after you've filled them with tiny gifts such as pens, earrings, candy, small toy animals, pocketknives, etc. Or do an inexpensive alternative and insert a special message in each cracker—a Bible verse, something you've appreciated about that person over the past year, or a promise to do them a special favor. Your crackers won't "crack" like the Victorian ones, but they can be used year after year as a special holiday tradition.

Sachets

Fragrant potpourri sachets make sweet party favors.

POTPOURRI:
2 cups cinnamon sticks cut into 1-inch pieces
4 cups red rosebuds and petals
3 or 4 sprigs of tallow berries
½-cup oak moss
30 drops cinnamon oil

3 or 4 lemon leaves
1 cup small pinecones
30 drops rose oil
30 drops bergamot oil

Mix together and let stand in a bowl in a cool dry place for at least a week; shake occasionally. Then pour into small bags made from Christmas fabrics. Tie the top of the sack with ribbon and glue pinecones, sprigs of holly, and fabric rose at the center of the bow.

Napkin Rings

String little jingle bells on a wire, using an empty paper towel roll as a form, and then tie a red bow on each one. Your guests can take these jingly napkin rings home with them to hang on their tree.

Homemade "Coupons"

"Give, and it will be given to you.
A good measure, pressed down,
shaken together and running over,
will be poured into your lap."

LUKE 6:38

For an
Elderly Neighbor

A book of several "coupons" that promise you'll add his or her grocery list to yours the next time you go to the store.

For Parents of
Young Children

A half dozen or dozen "coupons" that guarantee them a night's worth of free baby-sitting each month (or every other month)— or maybe a getaway weekend's worth of baby-sitting.

For Your
Children

An assortment of "coupons" that they can redeem weekly—for example, one day free of chores, an outing with you, a sleepover with a friend, etc. Or if your child is a teenager, you might want to consider monthly coupons they can redeem for the use of the car or an hour extension of their curfew.

For a Busy
Young Mother

A book of "coupons" for dinner delivered to her door. (Every time you make a casserole or a pan of lasagna, make double and freeze one, so you'll have plenty on hand.)

For Your Pastor
and His Wife

A single "coupon" that guarantees your help wherever they need it most—as a substitute Sunday school teacher, as a cleaning person, with maintenance and repairs, etc.

For Your Parents

"Coupons" that are really self-addressed, stamped postcards—each one with the reminder to spend some time on the phone with your parents.

For Your Spouse

A book of "coupons" that promises your mate an assortment of "services"—a back rub, a favorite meal, a night out together with no kids, help with a hated chore, a night out with friends while you stay home with the kids, etc.

For a Coworker

An assortment of "coupons" promising an out-of-the-office lunch on a stressful day, help with a large project, or carpool service whenever needed.

For a Teacher

An assortment of "coupons" he or she can redeem for help correcting papers, making copies, cutting out materials, or other classroom chores.

For a Busy Friend

Assorted "coupons" she can redeem monthly, promising her help with housecleaning, laundry, running errands, or meals.

Every good and perfect gift
is from above,
coming down from
the Father of the heavenly lights,
who does not change
like shifting shadows.

JAMES 1:17